EVE'S CHOICE

Discovering God's Blessing

Walter Graham

ABINGDON PRESS / Nashville

EVE'S CHOICE
DISCOVERING GOD'S BLESSING

Copyright © 2005 by Abingdon Press

This book is printed on acid-free paper.

Library of Congress Cataloging-in-Publication Data

Graham, Walter, 1944-
    Eve's choice : discovering God's blessing / Walter Graham.
        p. cm.
    ISBN 0-687-05786-8 (binding: pbk., perfect : alk. paper)
    1. Eve (Biblical figure)   2. Fall of man.   3. Self-deception—
Religious aspects—Christianity.   4. Bible. O.T. Genesis II-IV—
Criticism, interpretation, etc. I. Title.

    BS580.E85G73 2005
    222'.1109505—dc22

                                                    2004021634

05 06 07 08 09 10 11 12 13 14—10 9 8 7 6 5 4 3 2 1

MANUFACTURED IN THE UNITED STATES OF AMERICA

CONTENTS

INTRODUCTION   7

1. The Tree   11

2. The Snake   18

3. Into the World   27

4. Family   36

5. Heartache   45

6. Banishment   49

7. The Mark   56

8. Lost Lamb   60

9. Cain Returns   66

10. The Tree of Life   75

DISCUSSION GUIDE   83

Although she is but one,
she can do all things,
and while remaining in herself,
she renews all things;
in every generation she passes into holy souls
and makes them friends of God, and prophets;
for God loves nothing so much as
the person who lives with Wisdom.

The Wisdom of Solomon

INTRODUCTION

*E*ve's Choice narrates a plausible saga true to the Bible's text as it imagines how Eve, Mother of All Living, might remember and tell her story. It provides a fresh alternative to the traditional view of the tale as one of humanity's dark side. I have chosen to present Eve as the heroine of creation rather than as a disobedient temptress. I imagine her as a person who bravely pursued a choice that God initially presented to Adam (Man of Earth), a choice to move beyond the animal world of existence into the reality of human free will. By exploring plausible motives for her decision to eat from the tree of the knowledge of good and evil, I hope to show how Eve can be understood as someone making a courageous choice in favor of wisdom and growth even as she suffered the consequences of that choice.

I envision Eve's life in a way that supports a positive, affirming understanding of humanity and our relationship with our Creator. As she lives out her life, Eve comprehends the extent of God's providence and mercy, which provides an important softening perspective for their departure from the garden. She realizes that God had been foretelling blessings, not cursing them. *Eve's Choice* challenges the deeply negative doctrines of the Fall and Original Sin. Rather than a tale of damnation by sin and punishment, *Eve's Choice* is a story of moral development through choice and consequence.

It is my hope that people will enjoy reflecting in different ways upon this paradigmatic story from the Bible. I invite the reader to reconsider the basis for several fundamental underpinnings of traditional Christian theology relating to the story of the Garden of Eden. I have written what I believe is a positive, affirming interpretation of Eve, which bears directly on the image of women in society, an interpretation that I hope repudiates the harmful ways in which women have been regarded as a result of conventional understandings of Eve and her role in creation.

As Eve or Mother of All Living tells her grand-daughter about leaving the garden and about the tragedies of losing Abel to death and losing Cain to banishment, she communicates her understanding of God, whom she knows as "The One." Her story reveals that in spite of these tragedies, she has come to know that God offers love, mercy, and providence rather than judgment and punishment. The characters in *Eve's Choice* help us see that it is we humans who wrongly attribute negative characteristics to God, yet God remains steadfastly compassionate. As she nears the end of her time on earth, Eve concludes, "You must trust in The One's goodness. Listen for possibilities, not prohibitions; consequences, not punishments. Listen for blessings, Serah, not curses. Blessings. Blessings."

There are many people who helped me with this book. First and foremost, I thank my wife and spiritual mentor of thirty-five years, Ann, or as her family knows her, Ann Lynn. Cassandra Cossitt is a friend and colleague who helped enormously with the early versions. Professor Amy-Jill Levine of Vanderbilt Divinity School, whose incisive comments and questions helped me reshape the book into what eventually became the current version, was an important influence for me. Finally, I want to thank my friend and former pastor, Dow Chamberlain, for his support of this project, and above all, I want to thank my editor, Pamela Dilmore, who made this book sparkle.

Walter Graham

1

THE TREE

Out of the ground the LORD God made to grow every tree that is pleasant to the sight and good for food, the tree of life also in the midst of the garden, and the tree of the knowledge of good and evil. —Genesis 2:9

To this day, I have no memory of anything before that moment. He was lying at my side propped on an elbow, inspecting me. When he saw that I had awakened, the tiny wrinkles at the corners of his eyes gave way to a full, warm smile. I relaxed.

"At last. One like me," he said. "One with flesh and bone like mine."

He looked at an ox grazing nearby, then spoke as he glanced at a flock of birds overhead.

"Not them," he said. "They are not like me."

He turned back to look directly into my eyes. "But you are."

I saw that he was right. We looked the same in many respects, yet different in ways that did not seem to matter much back then. And so, Serah, with that welcome and introduction, my life with your grandfather, the one called Man of Earth, began its fateful journey. I wish now that he had known you and you him. Though I could not have known it then, he was a man of tenderness and compassion. Our life together was very full. It was a life you should know for yourself.

As he spoke, he reached for my hand, and I stood. "It's my job to be keeper of this garden," he said. "But I need help. We can keep it together."

We strolled through lush surroundings as he showed me the garden's wonderful delights, explaining each flower, plant, and tree with great and obvious care. At long last, we came to a clearing, and Man of Earth stopped. His proud smile had vanished.

"There."

I looked in the direction of his solemn nod. Two trees stood by themselves side by side in the middle of the clearing. Man of Earth pointed to the tree with branches drooping under the weight of hundreds of little balls sparkling in the sun.

"There is something you must know about this tree," he said. "It is different from the others. The Creator gave me important instructions about it."

"What creator?" I asked. "What are you talking about?"

"The Creator is the God that made everything—
the sky, the garden, the animals, you, me."

I still did not understand. "What's a god?"

Man of Earth did not answer right away. He looked
directly at me as he thought about my question.

"I don't know how to describe it," he said. "But
I'm talking about The One. The One is very, very
powerful and can create anything. The One is the
creator that made all of this. The One is a god.

"I remember," he said, "sitting near the river one
evening, wondering about the Creator—what it is,
what to call it. Suddenly, the answer was in my mind.
It was almost as if the words had been spoken aloud:
I Am The One That Is, and I will be what I will be.
Since then, I've called the creator simply The One."

I still did not understand. "What does The One
look like?"

"I don't know. I've never seen The One."

"Then how can you be sure The One really exists?"

Man of Earth squinted into the distance. He
closed his eyes for a long while before turning back
to answer me.

"The One comes to me."

He could tell by my expression that I did not
understand.

"It's hard to explain," he said. "The One just—
comes to me."

"Comes to you? How do you know, if you can't
see? Can you touch The One?"

13

"No. The One comes to me in my thoughts. But it's more than that. I know when The One is near. It's just something I know."

He continued to gaze into the distance, apparently lost in thought. Then he looked at me.

"There are other ways I know The One exists," he said. "By thinking back, I can tell when The One has done something. When I see The One's creations and remember they were not here before, I know The One has been present. Like when I saw you.

"I had been asleep, too. Just before I went to sleep, I thought about something The One had told me. The One had said it was not good for me to be alone. I didn't understand what that meant at the time, but when I awoke and saw you lying next to me, I knew that The One had been present and that The One had created you. Now I will not be alone."

I could not grasp everything he was telling me and was glad Man of Earth returned to the subject of the tree. He began explaining its special nature.

I must have heard only a part of what he said about the tree, or maybe I did not comprehend him. Perhaps I had simply chosen not to understand, because my mouth began to water as I thought of biting into one of those balls.

"You say The One gave you permission to eat from every tree in the garden? So, we may eat these, right?"

His response was immediate, imperative.

"No."

I froze, my arm just beginning its reach to take the fruit.

"The One declared that in the day I eat the fruit of this tree, I shall surely die," he said. "That goes for you, too."

My arm dropped, and my eyebrows furrowed hard.

"You will die? What does that mean?"

"When something is created, The One breathes into the creature to give it life. That's what happened to you. Before you were created, The One caused me to fall into a deep sleep. When I awoke, you were lying beside me. You were not yet awake. While I had been sleeping, The One created you. Just as when The One created me and breathed life into me, The One breathed life into you. Then you awoke and saw me." I took a deep breath and nodded slowly. For the first time, some of what he was saying began to make a little sense. I could at least remember waking to see him lying next to me.

"When that breath stops," Man of Earth said, "the life of the creature ends. It falls to the ground without life in it. It dies."

I looked back at the tree. I had begun to grasp why he felt so strongly about it. Yet I was still confused, and the little balls looked delicious. It was hard to believe something so lovely could hurt me.

"But," I said, "why would The One say in the first place you could eat from *every* tree in the garden, and then say something like that? And what does *In the day you eat of it* mean?"

"Listen. That's what The One said, and that's that. Stay away from this tree. It is death. We're not supposed to eat its fruit. Don't even touch it, or you will die."

He spun on his heel to leave.

I shuddered. The tree that had been so attractive only a moment earlier now seemed ugly and frightening. I could no longer bear its sight.

I called after him. "What about the other tree?"

Man of Earth stopped and turned halfway around. Without looking back, he shrugged and waved aimlessly in the other tree's direction.

"It is called the tree of life, but I have no idea what that name means. I don't know what it is for. We already have life. The Creator gave it to us. We're breathing, aren't we? And anyway, that tree is too close to the bad one for my comfort. I don't think we need its fruit."

He opened his arms in a wide sweep toward the remainder of the garden as he turned back to face me. His broad smile had returned.

"We can eat from all the other trees."

Man of Earth strode away, and I scrambled to catch up with him. A quick glance behind at the two trees caused the hair on the back of my neck to stand. I felt cold.

That was the only time we ever discussed it. I

found myself walking far out of the way to avoid even a glimpse of the forbidden tree. It had taken on an ominous air. Yet something about that conversation kept working in my mind like a splinter trying to find its way to the surface.

What had The One really meant in those instructions to Man of Earth about eating from the trees? Why would The One say that Man of Earth could eat from every tree in the garden and then turn around and prohibit the fruit from that one tree? Why had The One not said simply, *Do not eat from this tree*?

I was not there when The One gave the instructions, and what Man of Earth told me sounded odd. Something about it did not seem quite right. What had The One meant by that funny expression, *In the day you eat of it you shall surely die*?

Had The One meant that anyone who so much as touched the tree would drop dead on the spot? Had Man of Earth gotten it right? Or could The One have meant something else?

2

THE SNAKE

"See, I am sending you out like sheep into the midst of wolves; so be wise as serpents and innocent as doves."
—Matthew 10:16

*B*ack then, we were friends with all the animals—a content and peaceful community. The garden yielded everything we needed. We did not desire anything.

We would talk and play together with the animals. We were so close and so much alike, Man of Earth said he had even contemplated having one of them as a helper and partner before he saw me.

As each animal was created, The One would bring it to Man of Earth to see what he would call it. Whatever Man of Earth called the animal would be its name. Man of Earth would also consider each animal as a possible helper and partner. But he was unable to find a helper who would be his partner among them, because he wanted a partner who was more like himself.

The snake was my favorite. He was a great conversationalist. (I am afraid I could not say the same for Man of Earth back then.)

The snake and I would lounge in the shade, talking long into the evening. One day, we were discussing how the garden came to be there in the first place. The garden belonged to The One, the snake said, and it had been The One who instructed Man of Earth not to eat from the tree in the clearing.

"I was sleeping in the sun over there," the snake said. "Suddenly, Man of Earth burst through those bushes. His eyes were bulging. He could hardly speak, he was breathing so hard."

I imagined how he must have looked and began to laugh.

"Between gulps of air, he told me The One had spoken to him."

I sat up straight. "What did he say? Was it about the tree? Man of Earth told me of The One's warning, and there's something about it I don't understand."

"What did Man of Earth tell you?" the snake asked. "Did The One say you are not to eat from any tree in the garden?"

"No—just the opposite. Man of Earth said The One told him he could eat from *every* tree in the garden."

He nodded. "Go on."

"That's what confuses me. Man of Earth has almost convinced me that right after giving permission to eat from every tree in the garden, The One said something like, *You shall not eat of the fruit of the tree that is in the middle of the garden, nor shall you touch it, or you shall die.*"

The snake frowned and wagged his head.

"I doubt The One said that. I don't remember Man of Earth mentioning anything about The One saying not to touch the tree."

"Oh."

My voice trailed off. I barely heard what he said next. Perhaps Man of Earth had gotten it wrong after all.

The snake continued. "Man of Earth told me The One said, *In the day you eat of it you shall surely die.*"

"That's the phrase," I said. "That's the warning that sounds so odd. What does it mean? Is The One saying the fruit is deadly? That we will stop breathing and drop dead if we eat it?"

"No. I don't think that is what The One meant. You will not actually die when you eat it. You will become like gods, knowing good and evil. The One knows that."

"Then why did The One threaten Man of Earth with death if he ate from the tree? It doesn't make sense. Was The One lying?"

The snake smiled.

"No. The One wasn't lying. The One never lies. But you can't take The One's words so literally. The One's directives are very deliberate, and you must pay attention. You have to think about them."

Man of Earth, I thought. If anyone in the garden would take things literally, it would be he.

"I think The One was speaking in symbols," the snake said. "You won't perish physically. You won't stop breathing. But you will be transformed. The old you, so to speak, *will* die. A new you will emerge. And based on what I've heard, acquiring the knowledge of good and evil is absolutely breathtaking. It changes you forever."

As I think back to that crucial conversation, the snake may have said something else, something about Man of Earth being afraid of change, but I did not really hear him. My mind was churning. What did it all mean? What was "good and evil"? In what ways would I be changed?

Then he used a word I had not heard before. He said the tree was desired to make one wise. I would receive wisdom.

"Wisdom? What is that?" I asked. "And what does 'good and evil' mean?"

He smiled. "You are full of questions today, woman."

"I can't stop thinking about that tree and what Man of Earth told me that The One said about it. You know so much more than I know, and I want to know, too."

21

He nodded patiently. "The knowledge of good and evil will give you the power to make choices. Once you obtain the knowledge of good and evil, you will gain wisdom to make the right choices."

"So wisdom is . . . ?"

"It is knowledge The One has. The One understands things we creatures just don't get. The One sees things differently, which is why we sometimes misunderstand. It is a perspective completely different from ours."

I thought about what the snake said. So that was wisdom—understanding things the way The One understands them. And I could obtain that understanding by simply eating from the tree.

My heart pounded as I considered this new possibility. I was not sure what the snake was describing when he spoke of The One's perspective, but I had heard enough from both Man of Earth and the snake to know that The One's knowledge was far superior to my own. The very thought of acquiring that knowledge—that wisdom—was exciting; the idea of experiencing the potential change was thrilling. I did not know it yet, but in that moment of realization, my life had changed forever.

"So," I said, "Man of Earth was not given a black-and-white prohibition at all. The One gave him a choice. The One was not saying the fruit is deadly and we will fall over dead if we so much as touch the tree. The One was warning him about the consequences. But how would The One know how serious those consequences would be?"

The snake chuckled.

"Come on," he said. "We're talking about The One, remember? The One's knowledge is limitless."

"And, that's what I get if I eat this fruit? I get The One's limitless knowledge?"

He recoiled. "No. I said you would become *like* a god, not that you would become a god. If you acquired all of The One's knowledge you would not be *like* The One, you would *be* The One. The knowledge of good and evil is only a part of The One's knowledge."

"But," I said, "it is still the knowledge of a god."

The snake became very still. He spoke in a serious tone I had not heard before.

"I have thought about this for a very long time, my friend. You may gain some new knowledge, but it will not make you as powerful as a god. And I do not think eating that fruit will bring you contentment or happiness.

"There's something terrible in The One's warning. There's a quality about The One and The One's knowledge that I find fearsome. There is a heaviness of the heart I don't understand, which comes from having only a part of The One's knowledge."

"How do you know these things?" I asked. "How do you know so much about The One?"

"Oh, I was the first, my dear."

"The first?"

"The One created me before the other animals. I was to have been Man of Earth's helper. Because I was first, I have learned more about The One's ways than the others have."

"Why are you telling me?"

"Because you are Man of Earth's partner. I don't have the same understanding as Man of Earth about the things The One says. Perhaps Man of Earth is right. But what if he isn't? I think you should decide for yourself."

"Have you told Man of Earth what you think The One meant?"

"Yes."

"Doesn't he believe you?"

The snake sighed. "Man of Earth thinks I am angry because he did not choose me as his partner. He thinks I am being cunning when I disagree with him and try to help him see a different way of understanding. He even said I am craftier than any of the other animals."

"Well, you're certainly more perceptive."

"Perhaps. But maybe the reason he didn't choose me is that I am not enough like him. I don't look like him, and I surely don't think the way he does. Where he hears prohibition, I hear possibility. I am not being devious. I'm just different."

"Is this—what you are telling me—is this wisdom you have acquired from The One?"

"No. I have never desired to eat the forbidden fruit. Therefore, I have not acquired wisdom. I have not obtained the knowledge of good and evil. No creature has. But I have listened to The One, and I have gained an understanding that I offer to you now as my gift of friendship."

"Are you like The One, then?"

"No, I am only a snake. But I have lived in The One's garden a long time. I think having only part of The One's knowledge, the knowledge of good and evil, would bring sadness. Oh sure, even though it would be fantastic ..." His voice trailed off in a way that made me stop for a moment. Yes, I thought. It *would* be fantastic.

"But," he said, "without all of The One's limitless knowledge, you would not be able to see everything as The One sees it. I think that's why The One warned Man of Earth."

He looked directly into my eyes. He seemed troubled, as if something sad were about to happen.

"If the knowledge of good and evil were completely wonderful and carried no serious consequences, The One would have given it to us without a choice. You should think this over carefully. I think that choice carries an awful price."

Truer words have never been spoken. But on that day, he might as well have been talking to the wind. I had no idea then what he could possibly have meant about that price. Had I known, I might not

25

have done it. At that moment, however, it simply did not matter. Once I heard what he said about wisdom, my mind was made up. I had made my choice.

The tree was no longer an ugly apparition. It had become a delight to the eyes. I no longer saw it as an ominous threat. Its lush fruit was once again appetizing. But more than anything else I saw that it would make me wise, and I wanted the special knowledge its fruit would yield. I went straight to the tree, picked one of its glistening balls, and ate.

I sensed a presence and turned to see Man of Earth standing behind me. He looked at my dripping chin, and his mouth fell open without a sound.

"Here," I said. I snatched another piece from the tree and shoved it into his hands. I beamed at him. "Look. I'm still alive. We won't die after all."

He raised forbidden fruit to trembling lips.

3

INTO THE WORLD

God said, "See, I have given you every plant yielding seed
that is upon the face of all the earth, and every tree with
seed in its fruit; you shall have them for food."
—Genesis 1:29

I am not sure just how long it was before I
began to realize how different things had become. I
remember looking at Man of Earth and experiencing feelings I had never known. He must have had
some of those same feelings because he clutched for
fig leaves to cover himself, just as I had done when
I realized we were naked.

As I look back on that moment, I'm not sure
why we felt that way. We had been naked in the
garden and had never been ashamed. It was the
way The One created us. But something caused us
both to look for cover. Was it really our nakedness,

or was it our guilt and shame over what we had done?

I was overwhelmed by the realization that I had done precisely what Man of Earth had warned me not to do. An unfamiliar stabbing pain pierced my heart. A feeling coursed through me that I now know all too well as the flood of regret and guilt and shame.

I became aware of another new feeling: I no longer felt secure. I felt exposed and somehow open to danger. Not only did I want to cover myself, but I also wanted to hide.

As I slipped into the underbrush, I saw Man of Earth do the same.

Where are you?

Was that a voice? A faint and soft lilting sound, it was more like my own voice than that of Man of Earth or the snake. Was I imagining it?

Man of Earth told me later he had had the same experience. An inner voice had welled up inside him, pummeling his mind with unrelenting and demanding questions. But unlike the tender voice I heard, Man of Earth told me the voice he heard had rumbled in indignation. *Where are you? Who told you that you were naked? Have you eaten from the tree of which I commanded you not to eat?*

The One had come to us.

The One knew.

We knew.

Oh, what had we done?

I wanted to escape, to deny. I heard Man of Earth sobbing in the bushes. "It was the woman you gave me," he said.

The gentle voice seemed to come to me again: *What is this that you have done?*

"The snake tricked me," I said. "It was his fault."

We were such cowards.

We wanted to blame each other, or anyone else, for what we had done because now we knew—we knew we had done something Man of Earth had been told not to do. That knowledge brought guilt, and the guilt brought shame.

I was ashamed, and I know Man of Earth was mortified as well. More than anything in the world, I wanted to go back and undo what I had done. But I could not. It was a crushing realization. This was the beginning of what the snake had meant about the price to be paid for such terrible knowledge.

As I cowered in the brush, the snake approached. He hesitated, then stopped. There was a look in his eyes I had not seen before. I know that look all too well, now. Fear.

"You," I said. "You caused this."

He did not respond, nor would he come any closer. His silence caused my face to become hot. I balled my hands into tight fists.

"What is wrong with you? Why won't you say anything? This is your fault. You betrayed me with your promises of a fantastic new life."

Still, he would not respond. I stood, and as I did, he drew back, his tongue flashing.

I kicked at him, and to protect himself, he struck at my heel. Without a word, he slithered into the underbrush. Our friendship was over.

Man of Earth's eyes darted wildly as we left the garden. I had never seen him this way. He had been so sure of himself, so confident. Now he reminded me of the rabbit that made us laugh when it scurried from its own shadow. Only no one was laughing now.

My question merely made things worse.

"Where will we go?"

"How should I know?" he said. "I've never been outside the garden. Look what you've gotten us in to."

"Me?" I said. "You didn't have to eat it. So don't blame me. I heard you whining like the cat, saying I made you do it. You're pathetic."

Our first fight would not be our last. Leaving the garden had been frightening. We left the only world we had ever known and stepped into the unknown—alone. At least, we thought we were alone because we thought we had offended The One so much we now would be beyond The One's care and protection. Of course, we were wrong, but the moment we stepped into the unknown beyond the garden, our shame so distorted our thinking about The One that we were terrified.

We walked until the light began to fade. I broke the silence.

"Let's go to those trees beyond that field of tall grass," I said. "We can sleep there tonight."

We have lived in this grove ever since. It was here that The One helped us discover grain and fire and bread.

Would I go back to the way it was then, before that conversation with the snake? Even now, I am not entirely sure.

Were such a thing possible, I could have avoided the devastating heartbreak I would later endure. But without that knowledge, I would never have known what it means to love and to be loved, as I would also learn over the coming years.

The knowledge I acquired would eventually bring love into my life, and The One knows how heartrending love can be. It was a terrible price, indeed.

One night, as we sat by the fire that baked the bread we would eat before sleeping, Man of Earth interrupted the flame's cracking and hissing.

"Now I understand what The One meant about the plants of the field," he said.

"What do you mean?"

"On the day we had to leave, I heard the voice say, *You will no longer eat from the trees of the garden. You will toil to eat from the plants of the field. And you will eat bread.*"

He stared at the fire, lost in the memory of that fateful day. What he said next made me reach over and place my hand on his forearm.

"I was afraid," he said. "It was as if the very ground had been cursed. When I heard those words, I thought I would never be able to raise anything from the earth except thorns and thistles."

I squeezed his forearm gently and spoke my understanding.

"I thought so, too," I said. "But what did we know? We had no idea what bread was."

"Now, though," Man of Earth said, "I understand. We did not realize it, but The One was giving us a food far more wonderful than any of the fruits in the garden. I was too fearful and anxious to realize the treasure that was in store. Instead of blessings, I was hearing curses."

I smiled and nodded. I thought, too, of the great joy Man of Earth received from the fruits of his labor in the fields. And, my, how that man loved to work! Yet how could he possibly have anticipated such joy at the time? But just as in the garden when we labored together to till and keep its bounty, Man of Earth and I worked the earth to produce the grass we would turn into bread. And also as in the garden, our labors in the fields filled us with a deep sense of satisfaction.

"The One was blessing us," I said. "Don't you remember how the voice said we had been given every plant yielding seed that is upon the face of the earth, and we would have them for food? Though we did not understand then, The One was telling us to plant those seeds to grow grain for food, for bread."

Man of Earth looked at me and nodded his agreement.

"I know now I can trust The One," I said. "But on that fearful day, I could not do so. I was too afraid."

I felt the leathery touch of Man of Earth's hand resting gently on mine. I smiled into his face, and he smiled back.

I realized that I had heard that voice before, when I first awoke in the garden and saw Man of Earth next to me. The words came back slowly: *I created you both male and female. Be fruitful and multiply. My creation, including you, is good, very good.*

The One had spoken to me at the moment of my creation, telling me Man of Earth and I were equal parts of creation. The voice also told us it was up to us to help create even more people by having children. There had been something else the inner voice had said to both of us, which made life bearable outside the garden. The voice said my desire would be for Man of Earth.

Before I knew what good and evil were, I never had the desire to be with him as anything more than his partner in keeping the garden. The One had blessed our union in the garden. But when I acquired the knowledge of good and evil, I experienced new feelings and sensations that were the beginnings of the desire The One described. That desire has yielded happiness I could never have imagined before I truly understood what The One had told us in the garden.

The fulfillment of my desire for Man of Earth was more than the satisfaction of a hunger or a thirst. It was nourishment, bringing wholeness and contentment no matter how difficult or bleak life might seem. It gave me eyes to see beauty in what I would encounter. Even when the fulfillment of that desire led to the heartbreak I would experience with the birth of my children, it was a deep and meaningful blessing from The One that made life rich and satisfied.

As we held each other in bed we would laugh sometimes when Man of Earth remembered the inner voice asking him, *Who told you that you were naked?* But neither of us saw any humor in our condition that day in the bushes.

I know now this was The One's way of telling him it was good for him to be with me, sleeping as man and wife. It is a pretty good question. After all, no one ever said our nakedness was wrong.

The One helped us with that, too. Even though we had done the very thing Man of Earth said The One had warned him not to do, The One began immediately helping us through the crisis.

Just as we were about to leave the Garden, we heard the voice again. *Be fruitful and multiply*. The One was blessing us as we left, telling us how important it was for us to use the physical and emotional desires The One had given us to further The One's creation. We thought we were so smart when we found those two dead bears and cut off their fur to make clothes. But I know now it was the inner voice that gave us the idea. The One's protection is always present. I have learned that The One is, indeed, the Lord of life. That night, after we had eaten our bread and watched the fire burn low, we slept together more passionately and sweetly than ever before. It was a special night, a night The One blessed in the most marvelous ways.

4
FAMILY

God blessed them, and God said to them, "Be fruitful and multiply, and fill the earth and subdue it." —Genesis 1:28

I have produced a man with the help of The One."

With those words, I announced our new status as parents. Man of Earth had hovered and paced at the edge of the woods where I labored through the night to give birth to the little man who emerged drenched in blood and water.

Man of Earth ran to my side and fell to his knees.

"You have brought forth new life," he said. "You are surely the mother of all living."

Mother of All Living. I liked that name.

I smiled without looking up from our son. "He shall be called Cain," I said, "because The One and I have created him together."

Cain wailed until he found my breast. I was amazed that this little child of earth came out of me knowing where to find his first meal. As I drifted into sleep, I recalled The One's words in the garden after we ate the fruit. The thought had come to me as clearly as if it had been spoken aloud: *Your pangs in childbearing will increase now. You will bring forth children in pain.*

I had not known what those words could possibly have meant. Today, as I look back on that long night in the woods, I realize The One had not meant the searing pain of Cain tearing his way out of me, or the awful distress I would suffer in later years giving birth to his brother. The One had spoken of something far more hurtful.

The inner voice had not said I would now experience pain. It said my pangs would increase. At the time, those words simply made no sense, and they frightened me. Now, a lifetime later, I understand.

Four winters passed before The One and I produced another little man. His name was Abel. Even when he was an infant, I sensed that something in his future would bring us new ways to obtain food.

In certain respects, it seemed our elder son, Cain, was already grown, even as a little boy. When he was only four years old, while I was still nursing his baby brother, Cain took my place beside his father in the fields, planting and caring for the tall grass that gave us bread.

He was tenderhearted as well. In the early spring, he would bring me handfuls of violets from the fields. Like his father who had tended the flowers of The One's garden with such great affection, Cain loved the blooming plants of the fields as much as he did the bread grass.

Abel stayed with me in our home under the great tree until he was old enough to venture beyond the camp to play with our animals. His gentleness and love for them would eventually result in a new blessing of milk and clothing from the sheep and goats he would tend in the fields when he was older. We could not have imagined the heartbreak such love and loyalty would yield.

On the morning of that awful day many years later, we prepared to make our yearly sacrifice of thanksgiving to The One.

When the time came each year for us to harvest the bread grass, we would take the first shoots we gathered and offer them to The One by burning them on top of a large stone beyond the fields. We imagined the smoke giving a pleasing scent to The One. It was our way of expressing gratitude to The One for leading us to this place and giving us the blessing of bread.

Although he had accompanied us to the sacrifice

each year since his birth, Abel seemed troubled that morning.

"Mother," he said. "I want to offer something to The One, also."

"What do you mean, Son? You will be with us just as you have been every year."

"But you and Father let Cain take the grass to the rock and light the fire every year. He doesn't even like doing it. He thinks it's silly. And, besides, I never work in the grass fields. I want to offer The One something of my own."

"Everything is already prepared," I said. "Maybe next year your father and I will give you the honor of presenting our sacrifice. I will talk with him about it."

Abel's eyes clouded, but he pressed his lips together and nodded his acceptance.

We left the flock near the camp and ventured into the fields to meet Man of Earth and Cain. From there, the four of us walked the short distance to the rock where we would make our offering.

As we were nearing the rock, I noticed that Cain had fallen behind. I called to him, telling him to catch up to us. He blew out a long sigh and began walking a little faster. Abel's words came back to me: *He doesn't even like doing it. He thinks it is silly.*

When we arrived at the rock, Man of Earth turned to Cain, who was still lagging behind. "Where's the grass for the offering, Son?"

Cain held out a crumpled sheaf he had clutched in his hand as if it were a walking stick.

"That's no way to treat the grass we are offering to The One," Man of Earth said. "Go on. Place it on the rock and start the fire."

Cain slouched forward and tossed the grass on top of the rock. I handed him the hollowed piece of wood holding the smoldering coals from our camp-fire, and he dumped the embers on the grass.

As Cain stepped back from the fire, Man of Earth glared at him. Cain's eyes met his father's for a moment before he lowered his head and stared at the ground he scuffed with his foot. The two of them would probably have stayed like that until nightfall if I had not interrupted. I began the prayer we had said every year since we had begun offering the sacrifice.

"We offer you the first grass from our fields in thanks for your blessing of bread. May it be pleasing to you, O Creator."

We stood in silence as the fire quickly turned the grass to ash. When the smoke ceased to rise, we returned to our tree in silence.

Once we were back home, I noticed that Abel had slipped out of the camp. I smiled as I thought that he must have gone to find the tenderest new lamb in the flock for our yearly harvest feast when we ate our fill of warm bread and roasted lamb.

Man of Earth and I were baking bread under the

great tree when Abel suddenly burst through the brush. I am not sure if I did, but I may have laughed at the sight of him. It reminded me of another time long ago.

"Mother. Father. I heard a voice. I think it was the voice you told me about. I think it was The One."

I let the stick I was using to tend the fire drop to the ground. Man of Earth and I glanced at each other as we both rose to our feet.

"The One? " I asked. "Are you sure, Son? How do you know?"

"It was after my sacrifice."

"Your sacrifice?" Man of Earth said. "What do you mean?"

"I wanted to offer The One something from my own labors, so I took the youngest lamb to the rock and . . ."

"You offered The One a lamb?" I asked. "It wasn't the one for our feast, was it?"

The look on his face told us it was.

"There isn't anything I enjoy more," Abel said, "than the roasted lamb we eat each year. So, I wanted to share that blessing with The One."

Man of Earth and I stood speechless as he continued.

"I had just finished saying a prayer like yours, Mother. The fire was burning the lamb's body, and I was watching the smoke rise to the sky. It made me very happy."

41

Abel's face seemed to shine as if he were standing in the brightest sunlight.

"Suddenly, I heard it," he said. "I'm not sure it was really a voice, but I knew the words just as well as if you had been calling to me, Father. I even looked around to see if you were there."

Man of Earth moved closer to him and spoke in almost a whisper. "What did the voice say?"

"It said my sacrifice was pleasing and that I had done well."

"Was that all?"

"Yes. I heard nothing else. Was it The One, Father? " He turned to face me. "Was it the voice you heard in the garden, Mother?"

I knew The One had come to Abel just as with Man of Earth and me in the garden. My eyes grew hot. I felt drops rolling down my face.

"Don't cry, Mother. It is exciting. You should be happy. I am."

I took him by the shoulders and looked into his eyes.

"Oh, Abel, I am happy. These are tears of joy. An old, old friend has come to visit you. An old friend who brings blessings and peace."

A loud voice interrupted. Cain had returned from working in the grass fields. "When do we eat?" he asked. "It's time for the feast. Where's the roasted lamb and bread? I'm starving."

He stopped and looked at the three of us as if he had just noticed the intensity of our conversation.

"What's going on? What are you talking about?"

"Abel has heard the voice," I said.

"What voice?"

Abel stepped toward his brother to share his exciting news. "I offered The One my own sacrifice," he said. "Then I heard the voice. Just like Mother and Father heard in the garden."

Cain blew a short breath out his nostrils and frowned. "What did this voice say?"

"It said my sacrifice of the lamb had been pleasing and that I had done well."

Cain's face began to turn red and dark. Man of Earth spoke to Abel.

"This is wonderful news, my son. The One has blessed your sacrifice. This means The One is pleased with us."

I could barely hear what Cain said. It sounded like a bear's growl.

"Why would The One come to Abel? Was Abel's sacrifice acceptable and mine not? Did The One have no regard for my sacrifice?"

"Cain," I said, "in blessing Abel, The One has blessed us all. The One did not say your sacrifice was bad. Why should you be angry because your brother has received something wonderful? We should all rejoice with him." It was no use. Cain ran from under our tree into the fields.

Abel turned to me. "I will go after him," he said.

"No, Son. Let him swallow his anger first. You know how he is when he lets it master him."

"But Mother, I don't want him to be unhappy about this. I want him to share my joy. I should go to soothe him. He is my brother."

"Dear Abel. You are such a loving keeper of sheep. Are you to be Cain's as well?"

"Yes, Mother. I love Cain, and I am my brother's keeper just as he is mine."

Those words haunt me to this day. Oh, but that Cain had only felt the same way.

5

HEARTACHE

For in much wisdom is much grief: and he that increaseth knowledge increaseth sorrow.
—Ecclesiastes 1:18 KJV

Cain told me later that he had gone to his favorite place on the other side of the fields. It was a spot hollowed out among the rocks. A small patch of soft grass grew on its floor. He had loved to sit on the grass in that enclosure ever since he discovered it as a little boy. He had named it The One's Footprint.

He told me he had shouted his anger to the sky. It was unfair. He was the oldest. He should have received The One's praise first. He deserved it more. He was the hard worker. He was the one who had worked the fields to grow the bread grass. Hadn't he always offered the family's sacrifice?

He said he had stopped his shouting suddenly when he had been overpowered by thoughts so forceful and clear, he imagined someone speaking to him.

Why are you angry, Cain? Why has your countenance fallen? If you do well, will it not be accepted? And if you do not do well, sin is lurking at the door. Its desire is for you, but you must master it.

Following Cain's outburst, Man of Earth had returned to the fields to work. It was nearing the time when light would give way to the dark of night. All the talk of The One and sacrifices had made my work take longer than usual. I was so consumed by it, I did not notice that Abel had slipped away, too.

I thought I heard Man of Earth's voice in the far distance. I looked up and strained to hear. As the sound grew closer, I knew it was his voice. Something about it caused my stomach to begin to hurt. My mouth tasted a sudden bitterness.

I stopped my work and listened. Now I could hear him clearly. He was shouting between gasps for breath.

"Mother. Mother. Mother of All Living."

"What is it, Man of Earth?"

"Did you hear it?"

"What? Did I hear what?"

Man of Earth stumbled into our camp. He could barely speak, his breath was so short.

"Calm down," I said. "Get your breath. But hurry. What is it?"

"The scream. Didn't you hear it?"

I felt my throat tighten. My breath came in short gulps.

"Was it the lion that comes down from the mountains?"

"No, it was human. But I could not find where it came from."

I looked around and saw that Cain and Abel were not in the camp. "Where are the boys?" My heart pounded in my ears.

"I can't find them. That's why I came here."

Since the day we left the garden, I had never seen him as frightened and bewildered. We stared into each other's eyes, knowing all too well the fears that lay hidden behind them. He bolted toward the fields.

"I will find them."

He was gone.

The rest of that awful night is still hard to recall. My memory is clouded by a thick fog. Every now and then, as if blown by a breeze, the fog clears, and I glimpse a bit of that night. Then it is gone. But I will never forget how I felt.

The specter will never leave me of Man of Earth walking into the distant light cast by our fire,

47

holding Abel's limp, bloody body. I sat paralyzed with fear and grief as I watched Man of Earth pull one foot after the other in a slow, painful march. His eyes seemed as vacant as those of the body he carried. Like Abel's, they saw nothing.

I heard a deep, anguished moan that grew into a wretched, tormented wail and recognized it as my own. I remember holding my grown baby in my lap as I rocked slowly on the ground by the fire. My tears washed his bloody brow. My hair dried them away as I bent over to kiss his cold face.

Your pangs in bringing forth children shall increase.

There is something terrible about the knowledge The One has.

Oh, Lord, I sobbed, take this knowledge away. I do not want to know good. I do not want to know evil. Without this knowledge, my pain would end. I would not know the precious love I have lost.

6

BANISHMENT

Then Moses severed three cities on this side Jordan toward the sunrising; that the slayer might flee thither, which should kill his neighbour unawares, and hated him not in times past; and that fleeing unto one of these cities he might live. —Deuteronomy 4:41-42 KJV

A week had passed since Abel's death. To add to our pain, Cain had not returned home. We knew why.

"The ground cries out for vengeance," Man of Earth said. "The very ground that received Abel's blood."

I wept and begged for mercy.

"If you must seek justice, take away something precious to him," I said. "But please do not kill him."

"He must pay for this act of blood with his life," Man of Earth said. "His life for Abel's life."

"Then banish him. Take away the life he has here, with us. Send him out of our presence to wander forever. But do not kill him. I beg you."

Man of Earth did not know about The One's Footprint. It had been a child's secret place, a confidence shared only with brother and mother. The next morning, while Man of Earth worked in the fields, I crept away to The Footprint.

Cain was asleep, curled in The Footprint's corner like a dog sheltering himself from the winter wind. I whispered to keep from frightening him.

"Cain?"

His eyes fluttered. Recognition startled him awake, and he jumped to his feet.

"It's OK, Son. I am alone."

He looked around in a desperate, terrified search and saw that it was true. His lip quivered, and the fear in his eyes turned to tears.

"Oh, Mother. What have I done? I am so sorry."

The deep suffocating ache I felt in my breast the night Abel died returned. Now, it was for Cain. I knew the heartache and guilt he felt, and I knew there was nothing he could do to take it away. I also knew I was about to lose him, too.

He fell at my feet, weeping. His entire body convulsed as I sat and took him into my arms, whispering consolations.

"I know, child. I know. Be strong."

I held and rocked him as if he were the baby I had

once nursed. We cried together until the sun passed over us and began the journey to its evening home. I did not know I had so many tears left.

"Oh, Mother," he said. "What will happen to me? I am so afraid. I am scared Father will kill me."

"No, Cain, he will not kill you. I begged him for mercy. He is your father, and he loves you. He promised me he would not seek your blood. But you must leave us and not return."

He sat upright and looked at me with widened eyes.

"Leave? Where will I go? What will I do? I will be killed."

"When Man of Earth and I had to leave the Garden," I said, "we were terrified, too. We had never been outside. Yet, The One protected us and cared for us. The One will do the same for you."

"But The One is angry with me."

"How do you know that, Son?"

"Because The One spoke to me."

Just as The One had come to Man of Earth and me after we ate from the tree, The One had sought out Cain after the fight.

"What did the voice say?"

"It asked me questions—where Abel was."

Though I did not want to hear the answer, I knew I had to ask. Cain strained to hear me. I could not look at him.

"Where was he, Cain? Your brother? What happened?"

"Oh, Mother. It was an accident. I didn't mean to make him die. When he came to me that afternoon, I was still angry. He found me here, and I said we should go into the fields. I wanted to show him how good my own sacrifice had been. He never worked in the fields with Father and me. I wanted him to see the beauty of the bread grass we had grown and how much it meant to me.

"I don't remember how it started, but we began to fight. I pushed him; he pushed back. We fought until I pushed him so hard that he fell back to the ground. His head landed on one of the big rocks Father and I could not dig out of the field.

"The sound his head made when it hit the rock scared me. When I saw so much blood, I screamed and ran away. I was such a coward. But I knew he was dead. I was afraid."

I covered my face with my hands and wept again for Abel. My tears were for Cain as well. I believed him, and I knew his heart was broken, too.

"Mother," he said. "I never meant to hurt him. I loved him. He was my baby brother."

I nodded and took deep breaths to staunch new sobs. I reached to touch his shoulder.

"I know. And he loved you, too. He told me that just as he was a keeper of sheep, he was his brother's keeper."

Cain's face became as white as Abel's had been that night.

"What is it, Son?"

His mouth barely moved. He stared into the air behind me and spoke very slowly.

"That's what I said."

"What you said? To Abel?"

He looked directly into my eyes.

"To The One. It's what I said when The One asked me where Abel was. I said, *Am I my brother's keeper?*"

My hand slapped over my mouth to keep it from gasping my shock. He dropped his head in silence.

Cain looked up slowly before speaking again. "The answer was another question," he said. "The One asked me, *What have you done?*"

It was a question I knew all too well. I repeated it almost involuntarily. "What have you done?"

"Yes."

The One's questions will reverberate in Cain's soul every day for the rest of his life. Believe me, I know.

"But, that is not all," he said. "The One said much more."

I raised an eyebrow.

"The One said the ground would no longer yield its strength when I tilled it, and I would be a fugitive and a wanderer on the earth."

"You will be banished," I said. "You must pay for Abel's life with your own. You must give up the life you have known. You will no longer be able to stay in one place long enough to grow bread grass. You will be banished from our home, sentenced to wander the earth. Forever."

I choked out that last, sickening word and fell to the ground, weeping until I was exhausted.

I must have fallen asleep. I looked up to see that night had almost come. I thought I saw the beginning of a smile as Cain watched me sit up. It disappeared quickly.

"Mother, The One told me something else. When The One said I would be a wanderer, I cried out that I would be killed. The One responded by assuring me I would be marked for protection so I would not be slain."

I smiled. "Do you remember the stories Man of Earth and I told you and Abel when you were young? When we told you about leaving the garden? The One protected us and even helped us discover how to make clothing out of bearskin. The One led us here and taught us how to make fire and bake bread. The One has always protected us. You will be protected, too."

"But what mark would cause me to be left alone and unharmed?"

"I don't know. But you can trust what The One says. It was not punishment. The One was telling

54

you the consequences of what you have done. It was said to prepare you."

"The One was cursing me."

"Oh, no, Son. I know it looks that way now, but someday you will see that it was a blessing, not a curse. That is what happened for your father and me."

"I know. But you had not killed anyone."

"Oh, but we had done exactly what your father said The One told him not to do."

I stood and looked at the sky. "I must return to the camp. Man of Earth will be returning from the fields soon."

7

THE MARK

And the LORD put a mark on Cain, so that no one who came upon him would kill him. —Genesis 4:15

*T*he last time the dream came to me that night was just as the sun was beginning its rise.

Once Man of Earth had gone to the fields, I searched the camp until I found the sharp black stone he used to remove the skin and fur from animals that had died. I bundled the stone with bread and roasted seeds for Cain and hurried to The Footprint.

Cain was surprised to see me again so soon. But he was glad I had come. I gave him the bread and roasted seeds.

"I think I know what your mark of protection will be," I said.

"What?"

"You will be made to look so strange, you will be fearsome to all who see you."

Cain squinted. He spoke through a mouthful of bread.

"Strange? What do you mean?"

"I saw it in a dream that came to me three times before I awoke this morning. I brought Man of Earth's cutting stone to give you the mark."

His eyes widened, and his voice quivered. He shrank back against The Footprint's wall.

"Mother? What are you going to do with the cutting stone? Are you going to cut me? Must I bleed because Abel bled?"

"No, my Son. You will not bleed. But I will use this stone to change your appearance to make you fearsome."

"How?"

"By cutting off your hair so that the skin on your head shines through. A man whose head had been shaved would present such a powerful image, it would frighten any enemy away. This will be The One's mark of protection."

Cain's hand reached for the top of his head as I continued.

"I will cut all of your hair away until only the skin on the top of your head remains. Once the sun has toughened the skin, it will shine if you continue to scrape away new hair. Your appearance will be that of naked strength, of hardness and untold courage. No one will harm you."

I was stunned by how handsome he was with his head shaved. As I think back to that day, I realize why he looked so powerful—his aura was that of a mighty warrior.

We set out for the quiet pools near the river where the animals drank. There, Cain could see himself in the water.

As we were approaching, I saw that the lion had come down from the mountains. She had found food for her cubs and was tearing flesh from the deer she had slain.

When she caught our smell, she lifted her eyes and stared in our direction. Cain ducked into the brush behind the clearing, but I was unable to move. I stood still as death. Two mothers locked eyes. She crouched, preparing to attack the intruder who threatened her babies' food.

I felt again the strange sense of being different that I had felt the day we left the garden. We were no longer like the animals. Somehow, they knew it, too. That day, I had seen fear in eyes I had always known as friends.

Her growl snapped my thoughts back to the present, focused on the threat only a few paces in front of me. Cain jumped from behind the brush to defend me. The lioness dropped the carcass from her bloody mouth and stared at him. When he saw that she was not about to attack, Cain screamed at her and waved his arms fiercely.

The lioness did something I would never have predicted. She crept away, leaving her cubs' meal behind while keeping a wary eye on Cain. He ran toward her, screaming louder and swinging his arms in every direction almost at once. She turned and loped into the brush.

Cain stopped. He spun around and grinned in triumph.

"Look, Mother. I scared the lion away."

"Yes. With the help of The One's mark, you did."

He caressed the top of his head and laughed.

"The One's mark. My protection."

8

LOST LAMB

"Which one of you, having a hundred sheep and losing one of them, does not leave the ninety-nine in the wilderness and go after the one that is lost until he finds it?"
—Luke 15:4

*A*s soon as he arrived home from the fields that evening, Man of Earth could tell that Cain had gone. He said nothing; there were no words to be said. We ate in silence that night.

When the warmth had returned to the earth after the cold time when nights are long, I spoke of children again.

"There are so many new lambs, Man of Earth. You need a son to help you."

"How can you speak of such a thing, Mother of All Living? Why should The One allow another human to be produced? We spoiled The One's creation by disobeying in the garden. Creating more babies will only make things worse."

"But why do you assume all humans will be bad?"

"Humans *are* bad. You have seen for yourself," he said. "Our disobedience in the garden. And our own son's violence. What more do you need?"

"We are not bad, Man of Earth. We make choices, just as The One intended us to do."

"Choices? Murder is simply a choice?"

"Cain was not a bad boy. He made a terrible mistake. He failed to master his anger, and the consequences of that choice were ..."

"Mistakes? Consequences? No. It is evil, Mother of All Living, not choice. It is sin against The One, and The One punishes sin. Look what happened to us when we disobeyed."

It was of no use arguing with him that day. His heart still ached, and his mind was clouded by the grief of losing both of his sons. My husband, who had always been so loving and tender, could no longer see the good of The One's creation.

Over the years, Man of Earth and I both came to realize we had completely misunderstood what the One told us in the garden after we ate the fruit. At the time, we thought we were being punished. But we slowly began to see that The One had been helping by preparing us for life outside of the garden. Once we realized that, we began to understand that The One was continually caring for us in unexpected ways.

Knowing this about The One, we started to look forward to the days and weeks ahead with happy expectation. But the loss of our two sons shook our confidence that The One would always care for us and protect us. That crisis caused me to doubt that joy and hope would ever return. For Man of Earth, joy departed with Abel, and hope vanished with Cain.

Man of Earth's ability to see The One's love began to return the day the newest lamb wandered astray. It was late when I finished my work in the fields. Since Abel's death, Man of Earth had begun tending the flocks, which would often take so much time he would come home as the light was fading into night.

Man of Earth returned from the fields with his flock. "Mother of All Living," he said. "I cannot find the littlest lamb."

The new mother was calling for her baby in a mournful bleat that caused my heart to ache.

"I must find it," he said. "You watch the others."

Before I could respond, he ran into the coming night. I could hear him calling and whistling and sometimes could see him faintly in the moonlight. Finally, his shrill, distant whistle faded into silence. The mother's pitiful moan kept me awake by the fire.

As the sky began to turn from gray to pink then orange, I saw Man of Earth crossing the fields through the wet grass, carrying the little one on his shoulders. I could not tell if the lamb was alive. It did not move, and Man of Earth's tired trudge looked as if he were carrying death's burden once again. I stood and shouted to him.

"Man of Earth, are you all right?"

"Yes, Mother of All Living. Yes, we are well."

He lifted his prize high over his head, and it called to its mother. I saw something else, though, that thrilled my heart. Man of Earth was laughing.

When he awoke later that day, the sun had already passed overhead. The sheep and goats had grown restless. Together, we led them to the water where Cain and I had seen the lioness. The long stroll was almost finished when he began to talk about his night.

"I was afraid the little one had been taken as food," Man of Earth said. "But I kept searching because I had not seen any blood. I found it asleep on some grass at the bottom of a little hollow in the rocks on the other side of the fields."

I smiled. We walked on; then I turned to him.

"Just like The One," I said.

"Like The One, Mother of All Living?"

"Yes. You searched until you found the lamb, just as The One searched us out and came to us in our distress in the garden."

"Nobody is like The One, especially someone so imperfect as me who makes so many mistakes."

"That's not what The One said."

"When?"

"The day we left the garden. Don't you remember? I will never forget. It was the thing that gave me courage to go on."

"What, Mother of All Living? What are you talking about?"

"The One said: *Look, they have become like us.* We had become like gods. We had become like The One, knowing good and evil. That is what The One said. Don't you remember?"

"I'm not sure. Maybe. All I remember is fear and how worried I was about having to toil in the earth for food."

"Oh, yes, Man of Earth. Yes, The One said those very words—*they have become like us*. We were no longer creatures living in ignorance like the animals; we had become like The One because we had been given part of The One's knowledge, the knowledge of good and evil."

"But, Mother of All Living, you make it sound as

64

if our disobedience has been rewarded. It was sin, and we and our children were tainted by it."

"No. No, don't you see? Our experience that day was not about sin and punishment. It was about choice and consequences. The One's statement that *in the day you eat of it, you shall surely die* was not forbidding you. It was a warning. The One was warning you about the consequences of making that choice. A part of you did die. When you acquired the knowledge of good and evil, the part of you that had been clouded in ignorance died, and you became like The One, knowing good and evil."

"Why did he punish us," Man of Earth asked, "by making us leave the garden?"

"It wasn't punishment. But we could no longer stay there with the other animals. We were no longer like them. They were afraid of us. I could see it in their eyes."

He sighed.

"I don't know, Mother of All Living. You may be right. But I am weary."

"Last night was a very long night," I said. "You need to sleep."

"No, it is more than that. I am weary of working without a son to help. Maybe the One will help you produce another son. Perhaps we can have another opportunity to raise a family."

9

CAIN RETURNS

So God created humankind in his image, in the image of God he created them; male and female he created them. God blessed them.... God saw everything that he had made, and indeed, it was very good. —Genesis 1:27, 28, 31

*I*t seemed the torment would never end. He simply would not come out. I remember praying, "This is too hard. Please let me die." Yet The One did not grant my prayer. As always, The One knew better.

When I awoke, it was as if I were peering through a fog. Things did not make sense. Was I dreaming?

It seemed so real: my beloved Cain was kneeling by my side. Yet I realized that was impossible. He had been banished, and he had been gone for years. Once he left, I never saw even a trace of him.

As the haze of sleep began to clear, I saw that yes, Cain really was sitting beside me. He was holding the baby to my breast.

"Cain?"

"Yes, Mother. I am here."

"I—I do not understand."

"I was nearby on the hillside, and I heard terrible cries. It sounded as if someone was dying. I came closer and saw that it was you. The baby did not want to come," he said. "I came to help."

"Where is your father?"

"He is in the fields, tending the flock."

"Does he know you are here?"

"Yes. He and I have been taking turns tending to you and this little one."

My arms were so heavy I almost could not lift them, but I cradled my new son in the crook of my left arm as he continued his meal. My right hand trembled as I touched his soft red cheek. I could not take my eyes from him.

I said to him, "The One has appointed me to have another son, so you shall be named Seth."

I must have fallen asleep again. When I awoke, Man of Earth was sitting next to me, holding Seth in his arms. His face held a look of fear and concern that melted my heart. I smiled, and he tried to smile back through moist eyes.

"I dreamed of Cain." I said. "I dreamed that he was here beside me just as you are now."

He nodded.

"It was no dream. He has returned."

I closed my eyes and relished the joy of having two sons again.

"But," Man of Earth continued, "he says he will not stay with us. He believes that he must be punished for killing Abel, and he will return to the land of Nod as soon as he knows you are well."

I was not able to think clearly about what Man of Earth said. My thoughts were slow and confused. Why had Cain returned if he was only going to leave again? If he could return, why could he not stay?

"Where is he?"

"He is with the flock. It will be dark soon, and he will bring them back to the camp then."

"I don't understand. Why did he return if he believes he cannot stay?"

"He heard your cries, and he came to help. He thought a lion he had been hunting was attacking us. His hunt had brought him closer to us than he realized, and when he heard you scream, he ran to help.

Man of Earth paused and looked at the ground.

"When I saw him," he said, "I was angry."

"Oh, how could you be angry?" I asked. "Seeing him gave my heart such joy."

"I still blamed him for Abel," he said. "I had not forgiven him. I was angry that he dared to return."

"But you do not seem angry now."

"No. I, too, want him to stay. Perhaps you can convince him."

"What happened? What caused you to change your mind?"

"The One."

68

"The One came to you?"

"Yes. The One knew my heart. Before I could tell Cain to leave, The One entered my thoughts with questions, just as it happened in the garden. Only this time the voice did not rumble; it whispered: *Can you do it by yourself? Can you say that I have not sent him to help you? What will you do?* Man of Earth looked blankly at my face without saying another word.

"Was that everything The One asked?"

He blinked and glanced at me as if he had forgotten I was there.

"No. In an even softer voice The One asked, *Are you without blame? Must her blood be shed before you can forgive?*"

In the morning I was stronger and able to sit under the tree. I ate some bread and sipped water as I nursed Seth. Man of Earth and Cain sat with me.

"Son, why must you leave?" I asked. "It is so good for you to be here."

Cain stared into the distance without acknowledging my question.

"You could help your father with the flock and the bread grass until I am stronger."

He continued to stare.

Man of Earth sighed softly and looked away from me. He shook his head slowly.

"Do you think you are being punished for Abel's death?" I asked.

Cain closed his eyes.

"I did a terrible thing," he said. "I must pay for Abel's life with my own. I have been banished to the Land of Nod away from The One's presence."

"Oh, Son. I cannot imagine The One wanting such a thing from you. Did The One say this to you?"

"No. I have not heard The One since that horrible day. The One does not speak to a man who has been banished from The One's presence. I must leave so that my being here does not cause The One to punish you, too."

"Cain," I said, "I know you blame yourself for your brother's death. But I remember you telling me that The One came to you after Abel was dead and that The One said you would be given a mark of protection. Is that so?"

"Yes. But ..."

"It does not seem right that The One would stop coming to you after that. The One is your protection."

"But, Mother, you gave me the mark that protects me, not The One."

He rubbed the top of his bronze, shining head. "The One has nothing to do with me any more."

Man of Earth spoke: "Cain, perhaps it was The One who sent you to help us in the time of your mother's distress. Perhaps The One spoke to your heart without you realizing what you were hearing."

"I am guilty," Cain said. "It is I alone who is to blame for my brother's death, and The One has withdrawn from me because of that guilt. The One is blameless and perfect and cannot be in the presence of someone like me. That is why I have been banished from The One's presence, and that is why The One has not spoken to me."

Cain's bitter words tore at my heart. Not only did I ache because a mother grieves for her son's pain, but also the weight of his guilt reminded me of the heaviness of my own in the garden.

Seth had ended his meal and gone to sleep. I handed him gently to Man of Earth and moved to Cain's side, wrapping my arm around his shoulder. He tensed his muscles, but he did not turn away. I spoke in a quiet, soft voice to ease his heart and mind.

"You have misjudged The One, dear son. And you have judged yourself too harshly. The One is our savior and protector, not a punisher who does not forgive. You have allowed your guilt to rule your life.

"Guilt is The One's way of warning us we have done something wrong and need to turn back to The One's path. What good is your guilt once you have turned back to that path? It is of no use then. It can only destroy. Ask The One to take it from you. Give it away; do not let it master you."

He looked away as I continued.

"I have learned that my guilt tells the disgraceful lie that I am not worthy of The One's love. Unless I master it, guilt will turn to shame. That shame will block my relationship with The One because of my fear of being found out. Just as it caused me to hide in the garden, guilt will make me withdraw from The One out of shame. That is what you have allowed guilt to do to you. You have withdrawn from The One's presence because of your shame. The One has not withdrawn from you."

Cain's jaw tightened, and he stood.

"Do you think I have not wished it to be as you say, Mother? Do you think I desire to wander the earth alone with memories that haunt my every waking moment? Those memories are my curse, just as the banishment is my punishment."

I reached up to take his hand, but he pulled it away. I struggled to stand but could not. I fell back to the ground on my hands and knees.

Cain turned to say something else, but he saw how I had fallen and rushed to my side, helping me lie on my back. I looked into his eyes.

"Son, I have stared at the stars for many, many nights in pain, remembering the choice I made in the garden and the consequences that came as a result. There have been more nights than I can remember when I cried myself to sleep, pleading with The One to make everything the way it had been before. I know feelings like those you must have."

"But, Mother, you did not murder anyone. You only ate some fruit."

"It wasn't murder. You never intended for Abel to die. You told me yourself."

"Yes, but he is dead, and I killed him."

"I remember you saying The One had come to you that awful day and warned you not to let your anger master you. But you chose to ignore that warning. You let your anger master you. Your ignoring that warning was the same as when I chose to ignore The One's warning about the tree.

"That day in the garden," I said, "Man of Earth and I responded to our situation by hiding. We hid from ourselves. We hid from each other. We hid from The One.

"We also responded by denying and by turning on our friends, turning on each other, turning on The One. We allowed our guilt and shame to rule us, to drive our behavior, to color our perspective. In short, we allowed evil to master us.

"Yet The One responded with love by coming to us, seeking to help by asking questions that would help us accept responsibility for the choices we had made. Once we did accept responsibility, we were able to turn back to each other and back to The One. We were no longer allowing evil to master us."

Cain looked up. His eyes narrowed and his brow furrowed.

"The One did not punish us." I said. "We punished ourselves. The One blessed us. But we did not hear the words as blessings, because our excessive guilt and shame had allowed evil to master us. We heard The One's blessings as curses. Even so, The One trusted us. And through it all, The One protected us and showered us with love. The One is protecting you, too.

"Cain, please do not believe The One is cursing you. You have hardened your heart so that you can no longer hear what The One says to you. You have turned blessings into curses. The One's mark is a sign of protection, not a stain of guilt and shame."

That night I prayed until the stars began to fade into the coming dawn. I begged The One to help Cain change his mind. I remembered the way Man of Earth's heart had changed after finding the lost lamb, and I cried to The One for something like that for Cain. I wanted to give him my own understanding of The One. I wanted to *make* him see the truth I saw.

My prayers were fading into sleep as the first birds called to the coming day. Suddenly the soft, urgent voice from the garden was ringing in my mind. *Can he know without learning?*

I knew then that Cain would be gone. The realization was overwhelming, but I believed The One would protect and provide for him. Once again, I let him go without being able to say good-bye. Once again, my heart broke as I cried myself to sleep.

10

THE TREE OF LIFE

"For there is hope for a tree,
 if it is cut down, that it will sprout again,
 and that its shoots will not cease.
Though its root grows old in the earth,
 and its stump dies in the ground,
yet at the scent of water it will bud
 and put forth branches like a young plant." —Job 14:7-9

*S*erah, I am old and weary. I tell you these things because I know you will keep them in your heart and tell them to your children, and they will tell their children.

The One did send us a new son—Seth, your father. I believe Seth is the best man we produced. He has Cain's strength and boldness, yet he is tenderhearted like Abel.

You have your father's eyes, Serah. Just like Seth,

you see the good in people. You see their potential, not their shortcomings.

Seth is my cheerful one. When he was a little boy, we would play a game about his happy spirit. I told him his smile was so bright it reminded me of a sunbeam. I would say, "Are you beaming today, Seth?" And he would answer, "I'm your sunbeam today."

I think Seth's inner light might have changed Man of Earth's mind. Or it may have simply been the passing of days. Whatever the cause, Man of Earth no longer thought of himself so harshly. And the inner voice he heard whenever The One came to him no longer rumbled. He heard a softer, kinder voice.

During those days, I would ask him whether he thought people are good or bad. He would respond with the patient, sweet smile that humored my incessant questions.

"Mother of All Living," he would say, "what difference does it make? The grass must be harvested to make the bread. Is the grass good?"

I would smile as he answered his own question.

"Yes," he would say. "All of The One's gifts are good because The One is good."

He was right. All of The One's creation is good—very good. Like everything else in The One's creation, humans, too, are very good. Every time I would bring it up, Man of Earth would tell me the same thing. And he would always end our conversation the same way. He would say to me, "Mother of All Living, you are The One's most precious gift of all."

How could I not love that old man?

There was something very special I learned about The One that day in the garden, though I did not realize it at the time. It was this: The One loves me, and no matter what I do, The One will continue to love me and protect me.

The One loves you, too, Serah. The depths of The One's love and mercy are—like The One's knowledge—unlimited. The bounds of The One's generosity and care are infinite.

One of the most important things I have learned as I think back over my life is this: we must trust The One. We must believe that The One protects us and comes to us in our time of greatest need. We may not understand that The One is present or that The One's actions are blessings when they seem like curses. Yet The One is always with us, blessing us.

In the garden in my time of deepest distress, The One came to me and loved me, forgave me, protected me. The One made my life whole again. The One is my salvation.

Was my choice disobedience? Was it sin? Part of me says yes, but another part of me says no, because when I made the choice, I did not yet have the knowledge of good and evil. Is it sin when a puppy or a baby who does not yet know the difference between good and evil, right and wrong, does what it has been told not to do? I was a baby that day.

Was it sin? This old woman has wrestled with

77

that question every night for almost a century. After all these years, I have decided this: whether it was sin is simply not the right question.

I have concluded that there are two other questions that are far more important. The first is this: when I do disobey The One, what do I do? The second question, like the first, acknowledges that I will, from time to time, disobey because it is my nature. The second question, then, is this: when I do disobey, what does *The One* do? I know now that The One will always come to me. The One will always be there to help me. I must not turn away.

You would have liked him, Serah, and he would have adored you. He died before you were born. I do miss him so. That day was the most desolate of my life. The moment I awoke, I knew. His body of earth lay still as a stone, but the breath of The One, which gives life, had returned to The One.

Back when we were hiding in the bushes, Man of Earth heard the inner voice remind him that he is made of the earth, and to the earth he will return. *Dust to dust*, the voice said. Our lives on earth do not go on forever.

Knowing that, and having the knowledge of just how good life can be, gives us a deep appreciation for each life. Now that we know what good is, we honor the holiness and worth of life in others and in ourselves. We yearn and strive for the good. We repel the evil because life is so precious.

I believe that the absolute freedom to choose good or to choose evil is essential for us to be truly capable of love. The One does not want a race of puppets to manipulate. The One wants us to make our own choices, to love, and to be loved. To love means doing what is in the best interest of the beloved. Love is more than a feeling; it is a choice. It is the choice of good over evil.

In the garden, The One said my desire would be for Man of Earth who would rule over me. I never told Man of Earth the second part, Serah, the part about ruling over me. I did not know what it meant, and I was afraid. But after he died, I came to understand it all too well—Man of Earth rules over my heart even to this day. My heart is his, still.

He came to me last night, Serah.

Twice in the days after he died, he came to console me. They had been days when I thought I could not bear the sadness of life anymore. He appeared as I slept, and he spoke comfortably about The One and the garden. It had been as if he were there in the garden, waiting for me.

Last night, he spoke to me again. My heart has been heavy all day. After all these years, my desire is for him, still, and I miss him terribly.

He was standing in the clearing. But it was not the

tree of the knowledge of good and evil that was filled with beautiful fruit. He stood next to the tree of life. Its branches were full, and they bent almost to the ground.

He was holding a piece of fruit, his beard wet with juice. He grabbed another piece from the tree and held it out for me.

"Look," he said. "I have eaten from The One's tree of life, and I am still alive. Here. Eat this and live. Come and live here with me forever."

As I began to reach, I awoke.

Oh, Serah. I wanted that fruit more than I have ever wanted anything, even the forbidden fruit. The One's tree of life gives life forever. I could never have understood that before I ate from the first tree and became aware of what good and evil mean. I did not know what mortality is. I did not know how precious life and love are.

I know, Serah, there are those who say life's hardships are the fault of my choice in the garden. They say it was sin, and we have all become sinners as a result. They believe The One is punishing us, that The One has cursed humanity for a sinful nature Man of Earth and I brought into being through our disobedience.

Oh, Serah, do not believe them. Judge for yourself. See that The One is a God of love and fullness, not a God given to curses and punishment. When The One warns, know that it is out of love for the creation. The One is telling the consequences of the choices we will make. But they are explanations to prepare us for what lies ahead, not curses to make us stumble into pain.

My story is one of choice and consequences, not of sin and punishment. It has taken me all this time and countless sleepless nights to realize that truth. Finally, I have heard what The One has been telling me all along: *I love you, Child. You chose—I knew you would. You must choose. The choice is everything.*

So it is with you, Serah. You, too, must choose. It is my hope you will choose the abundant life The One desires for you. But no one else can do it for you; you alone must make the choice.

Despite the pain and heartache, mine has been a good life. I have loved, and I have been loved, and that is the most important thing in life, Serah. Love is The One's greatest gift, and it comes with the knowledge of good and evil that is now ours. That knowledge and the love it enables carry a terrible price. But without them, life simply would not be worth living.

The One has been good to me. The One will be good to you as well. You must trust in The One's goodness. Listen for possibilities, not prohibitions; consequences, not punishments. Listen for blessings, Serah, not curses. Blessings. Blessings.

For years, I have thought the reason Man of Earth and I had to leave the garden was that we had become different from the animals. Acquiring the knowledge of good and evil made us so different from them we could no longer live together as community.

81

But seeing Man of Earth last night made me recall something The One said as we were leaving the garden. After declaring, *They have become like us, knowing good and evil,* The One went on to say, *Now, they might eat from the tree of life and live forever.*

Before we acquired the knowledge of good and evil, we did not know enough to even want to eat from the tree of life. The animals were the same way, and that is why they could stay in the garden. Once we acquired the knowledge of good and evil and became aware of the value of life, it became possible that we might yearn for the tree of life's fruit.

But even though we possessed such knowledge, The One knew we were not ready to eat from that tree. We had not yet experienced the effects and consequences of the choices the knowledge of good and evil would bring. Therefore, we could not appreciate its true worth or be capable of experiencing the eternal life it offers. But I am ready now. I am ready to eat from that tree.

I am tired tonight, dear Daughter of Seth. More than usual. I suppose the excitement of seeing Man of Earth again last night has worn me down. I must sleep now, dear child. Perhaps he will come to me again tonight.

I love you, Serah. Tell your father I love him. Goodnight.

Discussion Guide

You may want to do a group study of *Eve's Choice*. If so, prepare for the study by reading Genesis 1–5:8 and the book *Eve's Choice* ahead of time. Use the questions below to stimulate reflection and discussion within the group.

1. The Tree (Read Genesis 2.)

1. What names would you use to refer to God? How might such names describe something about God's nature?

2. How do you know God exists if you can't see God? How do you experience the nearness of God?

3. Read Genesis 2:9, 16-17. What questions occur to you regarding the tree of life and the tree of the knowledge of good and evil? What challenges you or makes you curious about The One's instructions, "You may freely eat of every tree of the garden; but of the tree of the knowledge of good and evil you shall not eat, for in the day that you eat of it you shall die"?

2. The Snake (Read Genesis 2:16-17 and 3:1-7.)

1. How do you interpret The One's instructions and warnings about eating the fruit of the tree of the knowledge of good and evil?

2. What is your response to the snake's characterization and its interpretation of God's words as presented in this book?

3. How do you understand "the knowledge of good and evil"?

4. How do you describe or define "wisdom"? In what ways do you think gaining wisdom might change one's life forever?

5. What do you think about the woman's excitement about wanting to understand things the way "The One" understands them? About her desire to have the "knowledge of a god"?

3. Into the World (Read Genesis 3:6-24.)

1. Read the first two paragraphs of chapter 3. How would you answer the woman's question?

2. Read Genesis 3:17-19. Read the discussion about bread in chapter 3. How do you think the toil and sweat required in growing wheat and making bread contribute to a sense of blessing?

3. In what ways does The One continue to sustain the couple in their life outside the garden?

4. Family (Read Genesis 3:16 and 4:1-5.)

1. How do you interpret the "pangs" of childbearing? How does Mother of All Living interpret this memory of The One's words?
2. What challenges you or makes you curious about Abel's sacrifice being accepted and Cain's sacrifice not being accepted? What details in Mother of All Living's telling of the story might explain the way the sacrifices were regarded by God?
3. What connections do you make between the tensions that exist in the biblical story of Cain and Abel and life in the modern world?

5. Heartache (Read Genesis 4:1-8.)

1. Read Genesis 4:6-7. How do you interpret God's words to Cain? What do they say to you about contemporary life?
2. Think about the human capacity to experience loss and grief. What does the anguish of loss tell you about the human capacity to love?
3. Read the last paragraph of the chapter. What is your response to the thoughts sobbed by Mother of All Living? Do you agree or disagree with her belief that without the knowledge of good and evil, her pain would end? Why or why not?

6. Banishment (Read Genesis 4:9-16.)

1. What is your response to what Cain tells his mother about Abel's death? Do you think Cain's story is plausible? Why or why not?

2. How does Mother of All Living use her experience to identify with Cain's apparent guilt? What does her capacity to identify with him say to us about our capacity to identify with those who have hurt other people?

3. How does this scene present parental love? What experiences—either your own or those of someone you know—connect to parental love that Mother of All Living expresses for Cain? How might this model of parental love reflect the love of God?

7. The Mark (Read Genesis 4:13-16.)

1. How do you interpret God's decision that Cain should have a mark?

2. What do you think Cain's mark would look like? What is your response to cutting off Cain's hair as the mark?

3. What does Cain's mark tell you about God? Do you see the mark as God's punishment or as God's protection?

8. Lost Lamb (Read Genesis 3 and 4:25.)

1. What are your feelings and thoughts about the idea that "all humans will be bad" Do you identify most with the views of Man of Earth or with those of Mother of All Living? Why?

2. Have you ever felt unable to see the good in creation? When? Why? When hve you felt a loss of confidence in God's presence and protection? What parts of your experience indicate that God was actually supporting you?

3. What are your views on sin and punishment? On choices and consequences?

9. Cain Returns (Read Genesis 4:25-26.)

1. What do you think of Mother of All Living's conclusion when the One does not answer her prayer at the beginning of this chapter?

2. In chapter 9, Man of Earth tells Mother of All Living that Cain will not stay because he "believes that he must be punished for killing Abel." What connections do you make between this statement and our own experiences of guilt? What do you believe about punishment?

3. What experiences have you had or do you know about in which anger and blame have persisted for a long period of time? What were the results of the anger? Was it helpful or not helpful? Why?

4. What do you believe about forgiveness? About guilt? About God's response to us when we sin?

10. The Tree of Life (Read Genesis 5:1-8.)

1. What stories do you want your children and grandchildren or other young people who are close to you to know about your past? Why? What advantages or disadvantages do you see in helping them discover their potential? Their shortcomings?

2. How did Man of Earth's view of God change as Mother of All Living tells the story? What did Mother of All Living learn about God? How does her view compare with yours?

3. What is Mother of All Living's view of human nature? Of love? What is your view?

4. How is one to understand the Lord God's statement to Eve that her desire will be for Man of Earth and that he will rule over her? Mother of All Living comes to understand those words to mean something lovely, not domineering. How would society have been different had her understanding prevailed?

5. How does an understanding of the post-garden fundamental nature of humanity as either essentially bad (fallen) or as "like God" affect your understanding of the cross?